OFF
THE
PATH

OFF THE PATH

The Zen of Mountains and Deserts

Sydney Musai Walter

Sunstone Press

SANTA FE

© 2014 by Sydney Musai Walter
All Rights Reserved.

No part of this book may be reproduced in any form or by any electronic or mechanical means including information storage and retrieval systems without permission in writing from the publisher, except by a reviewer who may quote brief passages in a review.

Sunstone books may be purchased for educational, business, or sales promotional use. For information please write: Special Markets Department, Sunstone Press, P.O. Box 2321, Santa Fe, New Mexico 87504-2321.

Book and Cover design › Vicki Ahl
Body typeface › Maiandra
Printed on acid-free paper
∞
eBook 978-1-61139-228-9

Library of Congress Cataloging-in-Publication Data

Walter, Sydney Musai, 1935-
 Off the path : the Zen of mountains and deserts / by Sydney Musai Walter.
   pages cm
 ISBN 978-0-86534-122-7 (softcover : alk. paper)
 1. Walter, Sydney Musai, 1935---Diaries. 2. Walter, Sydney Musai, 1935---Travel--Southwest, New. 3. Spiritual life--Zen Buddhism. I. Title.
   BQ995.L79A3 2014
   294.3'927092--dc23
                              2013043966

WWW.SUNSTONEPRESS.COM
SUNSTONE PRESS / POST OFFICE BOX 2321 / SANTA FE, NM 87504-2321 /USA
(505) 988-4418 / ORDERS ONLY (800) 243-5644 / FAX (505) 988-1025

CONTENTS

Foreword	7
Acknowledgement	9
Spring	
Non-attachment and Cherishing (Rio en Medio)	13
Flowing (Cimarron Canyon)	23
Summer	
You Are This Moment (Lizard Head, San Juan Mountains, Colorado)	37
Flowing Into the Buddha Way (West Elk Wilderness, Colorado)	43
The Path is the Goal (Truchas Peak)	57
I Am This Beauty (Sangre de Cristo Mountains, Colorado)	63
Autumn	
Lessons in Impermanence (Bandelier National Monument)	73
Autumn in the Desert (Capitol Reef National Park)	79
Winter	
Disappointment and Redemption (Plaza Blanca)	93
Discovering Myself (Syncline in the New Mexico Desert)	103
Never Alone (Grand Canyon in Winter)	109
Epilogue	117

Foreword

Sweet is the lore which Nature brings;
Our meddling intellect
Mis-shapes the beauteous forms of things:—
We murder to dissect.

Enough of science and of Art;
Close up these barren leaves;
Come forth, and bring with you a heart
That watches and receives.
        —William Wordsworth, "The Tables Turned"

I have been wandering the mountains, canyons and deserts of Northern New Mexico since I moved here in 1979. When I first arrived, before finding work or a place to live, I headed off into the Sangre de Cristo Mountains for a two-week backpack trip. Coming back from that journey I knew that I had found home. Having lived in many parts of this country, the word "home" always evoked the place where I was raised—until coming to New Mexico and those two weeks in the mountains. My love for and feeling of connection to this place has only deepened over the years.

When I first moved here, I took up downhill skiing, cross-country skiing, and white water rafting, as well as hiking and backpacking. Over the years other pursuits have fallen away, so that only walking remains, and walking fulfills me. The earliest of the hikes and retreats in these accounts took place after I turned sixty. Before that I was too eager to climb the next peak, descend into the next canyon, get on to the next adventure, to bother with photos and reflections. Not that I think I should have started earlier. In his meditation on aging, *The Force of Character and the Lasting Life*,[1] James Hillman says, "The least reflected upon, most undigested life is very much worth living—and the purpose of life in earlier years is to live it. Knowing comes later." I would add that contemplation also comes later and my walking is far more contemplative now. I often hike with no particular goal other than to observe and receive. I stop to reflect on the beauty around me and to photograph it.

I go for all day hikes at least once a month and every year I go off into the mountains or desert for a solo retreat. For a week or more I camp on the edge of some wilderness, where I spend my days sitting zazen and hiking. Almost always my hikes include some off trail travel and often the entire hike is off trail. Where there is a network of trails, I stay on the trail, in order not to damage the environment, and I am fortunate to live where there is so much wild territory with so few trails. Some of the places I have found to hike have no trails at all. Trails go to places and through places; to become intimate with a place I must go off the trail. Off trail I discover the qualities, the textures, and the challenges of the place. I enter the place and the place enters me.

In summer I hike the mountains, in winter I explore canyons and desert, and spring and fall offer their own possibilities. These hikes are generally between ten and fifteen miles and almost always include some miles off trail. I have a list of people who have asked to join me, so I inform these folks in advance of the hike, describing the territory. Sometimes I have a few companions, sometimes I hike alone. Either way I have a day free of the roles and concerns of my life to be intimate with the diverse landscapes of Northern New Mexico.

I am aware that these wild places that I love, like the rest of the planet, are being impacted by climate change and environmental degradation. As these impacts increase, some of these places will be drastically, even catastrophically changed. I hope everyone who joins me, either on the ground or through these journals and photos, will find ways to support and engage with one of the environmental organizations that are working to raise awareness and slow, hopefully even reverse, the progression of this disastrous course. My hope for humanity is that we come to realize, along with Henry David Thoreau, that "…in Wildness is the preservation of the world."

Sometimes ecstatic
on a peak,
sometimes struggling
over broken rock—
always the earth
affirms my True Nature
and supports my aspirations.

1. Hillman, James, *The Force Of Character And The Lasting Life*, Ballantine Books, Random House, 1999, location 1673 in Kindle edition.

Acknowledgements

On my retreats I am alone. Sometimes I am alone on day hikes, sometimes one or more friends accompany me. I want to express my appreciation to all those who have been willing to join me in the uncertainties and discoveries involved in hiking off trail and in exploring new territory and new routes.

I am especially grateful to Karen Klinefelter for suggesting that I turn the e-mail I send to those who express an interest into this book, and for pushing me to accomplish the task. Without her there would not be a book.

I also want to thank Jan Harrow for her editorial suggestions. The text is far richer thanks to her influence.

Spring

Non-attachment and Cherishing
(Rio en Medio)

> *A monk asked Dairyu, "The physical body decomposes; what is the immutable reality body?"*
> *Dairyu said, "The mountain flowers bloom like brocade; the valley streams brim blue as indigo.*
> —Blue Cliff Record, case # 82

Impermanence is a core teaching of Buddhism. Everything is in constant transformation, and this universal change, not the limited identity I call myself, is my True Nature. When the awareness dawns that there is nothing constant or permanent to grasp, it can be unsettling, even unacceptable. The monk in the teaching story above may be coming to his teacher hoping to find some solid ground, something eternal to which he can anchor himself. Instead the teacher evokes images of the transient—mountain wildflowers that will soon fade and flowing mountain streams. There is no "immutable reality body," Dairyu is saying, give up your attachment to such an idea, accept that everything is in flow. At the same time, he is clearly expressing his delight in this flow. An early summer hike through two canyons of the Sangre de Cristo Mountains, near Santa Fe, New Mexico, poignantly illustrate this teaching for me.

Gambel oak

I begin my hike up the Rio en Medio through a bower of gambel oak, the early morning sun illuminating the new foliage and casting long shadows on the path. In the sunny meadow beyond this grove I walk through thickets of wild roses, their blossoms perfuming the air.

First waterfall

After about an hour of walking, I follow a second path that veers off from the main trail, taking me down into the river through a narrow rock passage. Hopping from rock to rock up the stream, I soon come to a grotto where the Rio en Medio arches out of the rocks in a graceful plume. I rest awhile in this hidden place, listening to the music of the falling water.

Second waterfall

The trail becomes much steeper moving upstream and the river plunges over several more waterfalls. The pool beneath one of these cataracts shimmers over a bottom of golden sand. Foliage is lush along the stream, with willow, alder, and several kinds of grasses growing in abundance. As I gain altitude, ponderosa pines appear on the slopes above me, and even a few aspen.

Columbine

A grand assortment of wildflowers appears within the lavish green of early summer—the foolscaps of red columbine, the delicate blossoms of woodland violets, trailing vines of lavender clematis, bright yellow arnica, the clustered white flowers of western wallflower, and purple bluebonnet and golden pea modestly hiding their sex.

Violet

Butterfly

    I climb almost two thousand vertical feet before the trail levels out. Here, at nine thousand feet, small meadows shelter within forests of ponderosa, aspen and douglas fir, where I am greeted by thousands of butterflies dancing among the fragrant wildflowers. Climbing almost to the top of the ridge separating the Rio en Medio and the Rio Nambe drainages, I meet the Borrego Trail descending to the Rio Nambe. Posted on the trail sign is a message from the Forest Service describing the dangers of walking through terrain that has recently burned. The Pacheco Canyon fire last summer spared the Rio en Medio drainage but spread into the Rio Nambe. I consider the dire warnings and set off down the trail toward the Rio Nambe.

Charred log and aspen

  The early summer flowers along the Rio en Medio are a clear demonstration of impermanence, and the charred forest of the Rio Nambe presents a darker manifestation of that principle. Moving into the burned area, however, I can see that the devastation is not complete. The fire moved through like a fluid, in streams and rivers, forming pools and lakes of destruction and leaving adjacent areas untouched. Quite a few mature conifers have survived, wildflowers grace the charred ground, and shoots of new aspens have sprung up around the burned trunks of fallen trees.

  When conifer forests burn, the first trees to return are aspens. Conifers require shade from the fierce high altitude sun in order to germinate, while aspens are happy to sprout in open, sunny spaces. Fast growing aspens are relatively short lived, forming what is called a nurse forest, where the slower growing, longer-lived conifers can take root. This forest is in the first phase of recovery and I hope to witness the subsequent stages during future hikes.

Rio Nambe

The greatest devastation appears in the streambeds. I notice this first on the unnamed stream that the Borrego Trail follows on its way down to the Rio Nambe. A channel has been gouged out by spring runoff and the lush vegetation that characterized my climb up the Rio en Medio has been scoured away, leaving only rocks, sand, and deadfall. I realize the full extent of this destruction when I reach the Rio Nambe. The burned slopes above the stream could not hold back the runoff from the winter snows, and there are places where not long ago the level of the stream reached six or seven feet above its previous high level. It is slow going here, over fallen trees and places where the trail was washed out by the high water, forcing me up steep slopes and across burned ridges. An enormous ponderosa, killed by the fire, crashes down into the forest a few yards away from me. Startled, I remember the warning posted at the trailhead and all my senses are on the alert.

I finally reach La Junta (the meeting place), where the Rio Capulin flows in from the north to join the Rio Nambe. From the Borrego Trail to La Junta is only about a mile, but due to the destruction of the Rio Nambe trail, it took me well over an hour to make the journey. From here I make my way across the Nambe on a fallen tree, to find the trail that climbs back over a ridge to the Rio en Medio. This area has not burned and it is a pleasant if strenuous climb up over the ridge and down to the Rio en Medio.

Rocks in the stream

I am exhausted after the long hike, much of it over difficult terrain, and with a stiff climb near the end. I wander peacefully down the trail toward my truck, stopping frequently to gaze at the stream flowing over rocks in the late afternoon sun.

The Buddha taught that accepting impermanence as our true nature will lead to the end of suffering. Hui-neng, the Sixth Patriarch and the fountainhead of Zen, emphasized non-attachment, and Dogen Zenji warned us in his *Genjo Koan*, "Yet in attachment blossoms fall, and in aversion weeds spread." We must cultivate non-attachment, realizing that existence is flow, we are flow. All that arises must pass and to try to hold onto anything will only bring suffering. However, non-attachment does not mean indifference. The other face of impermanence is cherishing. As human beings we are presented with the challenge of caring for this ephemeral existence, this exploited earth. In the archetypal symbols of Buddhism, Manjushri wields a double-edged sword to cut away delusion. His is the wisdom of non-attachment, fierce and unrelenting. Kwan-yin has a thousand eyes to witness the suffering of the world's creatures and a thousand hands to help them. Hers is the wisdom of cherishing. Let us accept impermanence with joy and cherish one another and the fragile web of life on this earth. The responsibility to care for this world and its creatures rests with us and we can only take on such an awesome challenge if we are unattached to outcomes.

Flowing
(Cimarron Canyon)

> *Spring with all its numerous aspects is called flowing. When spring flows there is nothing outside of spring. Spring always flows through spring. Thus flowing is complete at just this moment of spring.*
>
> —Eihei Dogen

Sunday

This week in Cimarron Canyon is unique, in that I have always gone alone on these retreats. Last summer I told my son, Dan, who lives in Seattle, that I planned to spend a week alone in the autumn, walking and sitting zazen in Canyonlands National Park. To my surprise he said, "I want to go with you."

Over the course of our life together, beginning with a backpack trip when he was six, we have shared many wilderness journeys. We have backpacked in the mountains of Colorado, New Mexico and Washington; rafted white-water rivers in Montana and Alaska; and discovered that we share the same enthusiasms—a love of wilderness, a propensity for wandering off trail, an appreciation for challenges, and a taste for trout fried over a campfire (in Alaska it was salmon). Then Dan married, fathered a daughter, started a business, and became far too busy to have time for wilderness adventures with his Dad, so I was both surprised and delighted when he asked to join me on this trip.

Alas, about a month before we were scheduled to begin our trip I suffered a stress fracture in one foot and could barely hobble around for several weeks. Without much faith on my part that it would ever happen, we agreed to postpone our trip until spring. When that time came, the week we both had available was in the middle of May—too cold for the high mountains and too hot for the desert. So here we are now in Cimarron Canyon, in Northern New Mexico, at around 8000 feet elevation, which should be just about right for this spring adventure.

Arriving at the nearly empty campground in the early afternoon, we choose a site on the edge of one of the small ponds created by a diversion of the Cimarron River. After setting up our camp, I point to some rock formations on the other side of the canyon and suggest to Dan that we might explore them. I don't believe I have ever made a suggestion for adventure that he didn't enthusiastically embrace, so off we go.

There are few trails and no camping allowed in the 33,000 acre Colin Neblett State Wildlife Preserve surrounding Cimarron State Park, which means a lot of wildlife and plenty of opportunities for off-trail hiking. We set off up a steep slope, angling across the fall line. Although we follow large animal trails when we can, deadfall and loose rock makes this slow going, so we find a ridge, a spine of rock, which requires some scrambling and offers magnificent views. There are already some early wildflowers blooming—the brilliant yellow blossoms of oregon grape, the delicate, drooping blooms of franciscan bluebells, and tiny white daisies.

Dan on the ridge

At first the going is difficult because of the gambel oak thickets, but we climb past them, through the piñon/juniper zone, up into the ponderosa pine forest. We climb about a thousand vertical feet and then head back down through a drainage that looks open and workable. I am surprised to find no oak thickets in this drainage and wonder why. Clearly, a lot of water flows through this drainage during storms. Do these periodic heavy flows keep the drainage oak-free?

During dinner we hardly speak and I realize that a shift has occurred. Hiking off trail we have entered this place, begun to flow with this place and with each other. We also both realize that our enthusiasm for this steep-slope hike has left us with sore quadriceps. I hope this will not interfere with our hike planned for tomorrow, up Clear Creek.

Monday

Undaunted by our sore quads, we set off early up the Clear Creek Trail. This is the most popular trail in the park, due to several waterfalls not far from the trailhead. They are not particularly remarkable waterfalls, in fact only one really qualifies, if by waterfall we mean that circumstance where a stream leaps clear of its bed and falls through the air. The other so-called waterfalls are really rapids, with the stream descending over steep, rocky beds. Still, like most hikers I know, I take special pleasure in walking along the flow of a mountain stream, and the more turbulent the more engaging, with a waterfall being the ultimate turbulence. Perhaps this pleasure is so keen because a stream is like my self. The stream is water, which literally pervades everywhere, and is called a stream when it is contained between the banks that create its boundaries. The water is a stream now, later it will be a lake, water vapor in the air, rain or snow, the ocean. I am like this stream, identified as Syd Walter or Musai Roshi by a certain configuration of boundaries. Buddhist teachings remind me that this is not my True Nature, which pervades everywhere. These boundaries that identify me will break down, dissolve, and the components of my self will take on different shapes, identified by new boundaries. To realize this truth, to feel it in a compelling way so that it does not remain only an abstract idea, is the fundamental task of Buddhist practice. The challenges presented by this practice seem to fall away out here and the truth of the Buddha's teaching emerges.

Daisies

Early wildflowers appear along the creek—the oregon grape that I mentioned earlier; tiny white strawberry blossoms (how sweet these little berries will be to the being that finds them ripe); a lone red columbine; and these mountain daisies in their rocky fortification.

The trail is only a little over two miles long and ends where two small streams converge at about 8,500 feet to form Clear Creek. From here an unofficial trail, still quite good, heads on up. We might even be able to make it up to Tolby Peak, at 11,500 feet.

Talus slope

As we climb, the trail becomes steeper, rougher, and increasingly faint. Dan has the good sense to suggest that we enter a waypoint on the GPS before the trail disappears entirely. From here the terrain becomes even steeper and more challenging. We have to climb over a lot of deadfall in the forests and across talus slopes. Talus, rocks of varying sizes accumulated on a slope as a result of periodic rockfalls from the cliffs above, present unique challenges. These slopes are too steep for moving straight up the fall line, which means traversing with a variety of rock sizes underfoot. Walking here is necessarily an exercise in mindfulness, as each foot placement must be careful and deliberate. Any rock I have chosen for support may move under my foot, which could result in a painful fall. Sometimes we can follow a ridgeline, which means scrambling over boulders and outcrops. Still challenging, this proves preferable to traveling through the forests and across talus slopes.

Absorbed in the challenge, we speak almost not at all as we cover this terrain. I once heard my Zen teacher say to group of us in sesshin, "All alone on your black cushion." This paradox of being all alone and yet with another applies equally to hiking over ground that requires this sort of complete attention. At one point I did turn to Dan and say, "I am filthy, sweaty, tired, sore, and scratched—and about as happy as I ever get."

By 4:00 pm we have ascended only another 1,500 feet, still 1,700 vertical feet below Tolby Peak. I am always reluctant to turn back before reaching an intended goal, and over this difficult terrain there is just not time to make it to the top today. Descending a steep talus slope is no less challenging than ascending, and actually more dangerous. A fall on the way up is a fall into the hillside, but a fall going down can easily mean a tumble down over punishing rocks. We make it safely to the waypoint where we pick up the official trail and we are back at the truck about 6:30. How many miles we walked would be difficult to estimate, and almost ten hours on and off trail has left us exhausted.

Tuesday

We decide to spend the day in camp, recovering from the hikes of Sunday and Monday. We were warned that the water in the park is not currently potable, so we drive to Ute Park, on the eastern edge of the park, to fill our water jugs and to pick up more beer. The only gas station/convenience store in Ute Park is closed, and we have to drive twenty miles more, to a roadhouse advertising itself as "Cold Beer, NM."

Back in camp with our water and beer, we make lunch while clouds move in and thunder rumbles. Dan heads off to the river, to see if he can catch some fish for dinner; I sit zazen under a juniper. I feel only a few drops of rain while sitting, and coming out from under the dense foliage of the tree I am surprised to see how much rain has fallen. Dan is back now from his fishing expedition with several pan-size trout, all nicely cleaned and ready to fry. We will feast tonight.

I am spending considerably less time on my black cushion than I would if I were alone on this trip. Zazen is the core of Zen practice and although I am an ordained Zen Buddhist priest I lead a lay life. There are many of us like this in the West and we deal with an ongoing challenge: how to maintain an intensive practice of zazen and, at the same time, involve ourselves fully in the rich web of relationships that lay life creates.

I think we have found the best time of year to camp here. A ranger told us the campground fills up in summer with campers escaping the Texas heat and looking for trout streams. Now we have the campground to ourselves and the weather is mostly sunny, temperature in the 70's. It is ideal weather for hiking and we are finding no one in the backcountry, on or off the trails. The earliest wildflowers are blooming and the cottonwoods are showing a pale, green haze of just opening leaves.

3:00 pm

A man rode in on a bicycle a short time ago, towing a small trailer. The speed and efficiency with which he set up his tent let me know that he was accustomed to this routine. I decide to walk over to make his acquaintance and encounter a sixty-nine year old man, apparently very fit, with skin like old leather and not too many teeth. I ask him where he is from.

"Seattle."

"Seattle! My son is from Seattle."

"Yeah, but this bike has been my home since two thousand seven."

I learn that his name is Paul and that he is a Vietnam vet. In the winter he travels through the South, then moves north with the sun. I wondered how many miles he had ridden in the seven years that he had been on the road. He said he really didn't know, then pointed to the tire on the one-wheel trailer he pulls behind his bike.

"See that tire?"

I nodded.

"I had to replace that tire a few months ago. It had twenty-five thousand miles on it."

As our conversation continues, he says to me, "I sure am talking a lot today," and I have the impression of a man who spends most of his time alone and in silence. A lonely man perhaps, but not, I imagine, an unhappy one.

The stream flowing into our pond

  The tantalizing smell of trout frying over a campfire whets our appetite and we eat our fill of the pond's offering. After dinner and camp cleanup, I make some hot chocolate and we decide to enjoy it sitting at the edge of this friendly little body of water. It seems to be dinnertime here, with trout dimpling the surface, occasionally even jumping clear of the water in their enthusiasm. A muskrat patrols the edges of the pond then zigzags up through the rapids that flow into it. Above us, in the twilight sky, a few bats are darting about, and a flock of swallows appears, wheeling and diving for their evening meal.

  Reflective in the afterglow, we dream tomorrow. We plan to walk up Maverick Canyon, then off-trail to a 9,200 foot knob, and back along the top of the Palisades, the steep cliffs along the Cimarron River.

Wednesday

Heading up Maverick Canyon early in the morning, on an abandoned and deteriorating road, we see a turkey moving through the grass. A lot of turkeys forage through these canyons and sometimes when we're walking off-trail, one will explode out of the underbrush a few feet away, startling us with a tremendous whirring of wings.

After a mile or so the road becomes impassable with deadfall and we continue on up off- trail. This entire drainage is crisscrossed with a network of old logging roads. I don't know when it was logged and it was not clearcut, since relatively few trees were selected. Judging from the conifers and oaks growing in the eroded roadbeds, the logging took place many years ago.

We spot an elk as we make our way up, a cow or a young bull. Later a four-legged creature the size of a fox or bobcat darts through the forest too quickly to be positively identified. When we examine what we believe to be this creature's tracks, we notice that the claws had not been retracted, as they would have been on a feline, so it was probably a fox. Still later a falcon swoops through the woods just over our heads. We eat lunch on a knob at about 9,400 feet, while dark clouds hover nearby and thunder rumbles. A light rain sprinkles us, then the storm rolls off in another direction.

6:00 pm

Dan is fishing as I write this, so I imagine we will have trout for dinner again tonight. He has become intimate with this pond and its stream. He'll fish for a while, then sit to observe the comings and goings of the rich web of life that the water makes possible.

Returning with his catch, he reports how the trout are behaving, what the muskrat is up to, the occasional appearance of a duck. He describes his concern for a little bird that hopped from rock to rock in the rapids, fearing that it might fall into the stream. Then, to his amazement, the bird dove into the water. The bird he expressed such concern for is a Water Ouzel, or Dipper, so named for the way it bobs up and down while standing. The dipper not only dives for its food of water plants, crustaceans, and small fish, it can actually walk along the bottom of a stream, searching for a meal.

Dan is the ideal camping/hiking companion. His curiosity is boundless, he never complains, he is up for any challenge, and he is always ready to take on his share of the chores involved in camping.

Thursday

I find some landforms compelling, they seem to pull at me, urging me to enter and explore. Ever since I drove through here on my way back from a meeting in Colorado earlier this year, I've dreamed of hiking up one of the steep drainages coming down through the Palisade Cliffs and walking along the top of that formation. Today Dan and I have driven to one of these drainages to fulfill that dream. Not long after we start up we discover that we are on a long abandoned four-wheel-drive roadbed that ends after a mile or two at a small spring. An old cast iron pipe pokes out of the hillside, so someone, sometime, tapped this spring for fresh water. Whoever it was is long gone, but the water still flows, and as spring turns to summer a garden of grasses and wildflowers will thrive here.

From the trailhead at 7,700 feet, we follow the drainage up to its head and then on up to a knob at 9,200 feet. A well-used elk trail facilitates our way up the slope. Elk are big animals and their passage keeps trails clear of brush and trees that would otherwise make walking difficult. We scramble up to the top of the cliffs, then walk along the edge, which is much higher than it appears from the canyon bottom. From the riverbed the cliffs appear to be only about three hundred feet high, but the steep slopes that we have climbed and the high cliffs where we walk now are hidden from that vantage point.

West from the top of the cliffs

The tops of the cliffs look like the ruined battlements of an old fortress. From here we can look west to the Wheeler Peak Range where snow still lingers on the high peaks, east to Eagle Nest Lake, and down along precipitous rock faces. A strong breeze up here, with powerful gusts, fortunately pushes us back from, rather than toward the danger of the cliff edge. There are no trails, so we follow the edge of the cliffs, making our way through drainages and across ridges back to our camp.

Cimarron River at the Palisades

Back at camp, hot and tired from our day on the cliffs, we face a two-mile walk to the truck, parked at the trailhead where we began the hike. Dan offers to go alone and I take him up on his offer, so that I can sit zazen below the cliffs, in sunlight filtered through the foliage of a ponderosa, listening to the voices of the river and cooled by a light breeze.

Friday

After breakfast we break camp and pack up to head back to Santa Fe. We flow together easily in these tasks, as we have throughout the trip, re-establishing a special connection between us. I have many concerns and difficulties in my life in Santa Fe. I am sure the same is true for Dan in Seattle. For this week we have spent together in Cimarron Canyon those concerns vanished, replaced by concerns such as how to make our way with no trail, where to place the next foot on a steep talus slope, how to prepare a meal in the rain. We have lived in the present, depending on each other, encountering the place, flowing.

> "In your study of flowing, if you imagine the objective to be outside yourself and that you flow and move through hundreds and thousands of worlds, for hundreds, thousands, and myriads of eons, you have not devotedly studied the buddha way."
>
> —Eihei Dogen

Summer

You Are This Moment
(Lizard Head Wilderness, San Juan Mountains, Colorado)

> *The birds have vanished down the sky.*
> *Now the last cloud drains away.*
> *We sit together, the mountain and me,*
> *until only the mountain remains.*
> —Li Po

Sunday

It's overcast as I leave my campsite and set out on the Fall Creek trail. I have a solemn feeling when I begin a hike with rain threatening, quite different from the exuberance I feel when I set out in fair weather. Following switchbacks up the steep trail through a forest of spruce and fir, the rain never materializes. I stop on a ridge at timberline, exulting in the strong wind driving clouds across the hump of Johnny Bull Mountain to the South and the massive group of summits dominated by Dolores and Dunn Peaks to the North. With the wind and threatening rain, I have the mountain to myself, and my solo retreat seems well begun. On the way back to camp I stop to watch a bull elk bounding across a huge, lush meadow.

Monday

The sun is shining on me as I start up toward the saddle between the upthrust column of rock that is Lizard Head and the gentle curve of Cross Mountain, and I can see clouds rolling across the ridge between the two summits. I climb for an hour and a half up through the uniformity of a conifer forest. Hiking through conifers is much like sitting meditation—nothing changes except my mind.

Low clouds move in, alternately covering and revealing the sun. I am always surprised by how quickly my moods change out here, depending on changes in the weather. I can feel quite somber under an overcast sky and a moment later be flooded with happiness when the sun emerges.

Clouds across the mountains

    One and a half hours brings me to fewer trees and small meadows, and in two hours I am above timberline, at the base of thirteen thousand foot summits. To the west, lush, green meadows, studded with alpine wildflowers sweep up to Cross Mountain, and heavy clouds loom over Mount Wilson in the distance. The view to the north is obscured by mist so I stop to study my map and pinpoint my location. When I look up again, there is the soaring prominence of Lizard head emerging from the clouds.

Lizard Head in the clouds

    I continue on up to the saddle between Lizard Head and Cross Mountain through the meadows, where alpine versions of paintbrush, daisies, buttercups, purple fringe and a multitude of flowers I cannot name present a full spectrum of color among the boulders. I have the trail to myself all morning and when I meet another hiker at the saddle we exchange less than a dozen words, both, I think, valuing our solitude. I linger on the ridge, letting the vista of peaks and the high mountain air fill me. I consider climbing another five or six hundred vertical feet, to where the upper slope of Lizard Head becomes a sheer face, but a squall sweeps through so I slip on my poncho and head back down. When I reach the trailhead I sit for a long while inside my truck, with the rain falling softly, filled with the deep peace and joy that these hikes above timberline bring me.

Tuesday

I spend the morning in sitting meditation. How wonderful to let go of everything, to let go of all my stories, in the deep absorption of zazen. Our stories about the world and ourselves are all that maintain the illusion of self and letting go of the stories all that is required for liberation.

So many of the supports for a sense of self are missing out here. No work, no relationships, no packaged entertainment. In the simplicity of life reduced to basics, a deep sense of peace and contentment emerges. Emotions arise and pass away, both stronger and more ephemeral than when I am going about my usual routines. Joy and sorrow and all the lesser manifestations of these feelings visit me for a while and vanish, coming and going like the light and the dark, the sun and the rain.

INSTRUCTIONS FOR ZAZEN

Nothing to be done.
No fear, hope, regret.
No dreams,
and no broken dreams.
When these arise,
view them as mist
arising from a lake at daybreak,
dissipating in the sun.
This moment is birth and death.
You are this moment.

Rain every day, and the low clouds look as though they will bring more today. Sometimes it begins before noon, sometimes not till four or five pm; sometimes slow and steady, sometimes a downpour, with thunder and lightning. Having to deal with the rain every day, and not knowing just when it will happen, certainly promotes mindfulness.

Wednesday

A strenuous hike up to Navajo Lake today. Rather gentle up hill trail for the first two miles, much of it through lush meadows fed by the abundant rains here. Yellow sunflowers as tall as I am, blue larkspur, white corn lilies and cow parsnips higher still.

The last two miles of trail are mostly switchbacks up the steep slope to Navajo Basin. I am very slow now on these uphill stretches at high altitude. My progress is meditative—one step, one step.

Navajo Lake

Navajo Lake is so lovely. Fringed with wildflowers and small conifers, it sits in an alpine basin beneath towering, snow covered Mount Wilson. As soon as I arrive at the lake it begins to rain, so I retreat to the shelter of a spruce tree, put on my poncho, and eat lunch. I sit contentedly beneath the protection of my tree for quite some time, while the rain and hail pound down. When the storm lets up I start back, and not long after the sun comes out, warming and drying me on the way down.

Because I left the trailhead early this morning I had the trail to myself going up. Coming down, I pass a few hikers and backpackers heading up. I feel some nostalgia, wistfulness, seeing these young people, with their strong bodies and backpacks, striding up sections of trail where my pace is so slow that it becomes kinhin, the slow walking meditation of Zen.

Thursday

It would be difficult to overstate how blessed I feel by these retreats. In my life, except perhaps during zazen, I am always someone. I take up the roles of husband, father, psychotherapist, Zen teacher, and more. Out here I am no one. The mountains, which offer me such extraordinary beauty, challenge, and adventure, set the terms of these encounters. The place is utterly indifferent to me and to my well-being. I have no standing, and if I do not recognize, accept and pay attention to the terms set by the mountains I will be injured or dead.

These peaks, meadows, streams, and forests, are who I am, yet, at the same time, I am separate from and permeated by them. When body and mind are completely engaged I am free of self, I am just this. When I experience myself as separate from and within this place, the wilderness infuses body and mind, down to the level of my cells, with its beauty and magnificence.

Flowing Into the Buddha Way
(West Elk Wilderness, Colorado)

> *There are those who, attracted by grass, flowers,*
> *mountains, and waters, flow into the buddha way.*
> —Dogen, "Bendowa"

Sunday

As the limitations, infirmities, and indignities of aging degrade my body and mind at an ever increasing pace, I can feel the pull of comfort and safety, of known places, people, and situations. I am not ready to surrender to this pull. I still want difficulty, challenge, surprise, and for me that means finding another mountain to climb and another desert to explore. They do not always have to be new mountains and deserts. Those places I have already visited offer different difficulties, challenges, and surprises each time I encounter them, especially when I travel off trail. I still want to wander in wild places, to be intimate with grass, flowers, mountains, and waters, to flow into the buddha way.

At the height of summer I'm setting out for another solo retreat in the Colorado Rockies, this time to Lost Lake, west of Crested Butte. A small campground there, situated between the Raggeds and West Elk Wildernesses, promises hikes through some intriguing terrain.

Once through Espanola, Hiway 84/285 divides, and 285 takes me up along the dark hulk of Black Mesa onto the high plains of Northern New Mexico. Almost no traffic on this road over rolling hills, and I begin to experience myself alone, each mile creating more separation between myself and all the relationships of my life in Santa Fe.

The transition from New Mexico to Colorado at Antonito is dramatic. The empty sagebrush flats and forested hills of Northern New Mexico give way to the enormous, irrigated fields and tacky commercial strips of the San Luis Valley. Cumulus clouds tower over the mountain ranges on either side of this wide valley, their brilliant whiteness a breathtaking sight against the intensely blue sky. A magnificent spectacle from this distance, and under those clouds I can see, here and there, heavy rain falling. I will probably have to cope with some of this rain on my retreat and my experience of the clouds from that perspective will be quite different.

Leaving the little town of Saguache, I begin climbing into the foothills of the Rio Grande National Forest. Fortress-like rock formations loom above the road. Lush forests of dark conifers and bright green aspens replace the cultivated fields of the San Luis Valley. Heading toward Cochetopa Pass, I drive in and out of heavy rain, which stops abruptly on the other side of pass, the sun breaking through the cloud cover. From the pass the road descends on tight curves between the sheer rock walls of Cochetopa Canyon into Gunnison, where I will spend the night in a motel before setting off for Lost Lake.

Monday

Awakening early to a cloudless sky, I am on the Kebler Pass road, out of Crested Butte, before seven am. Arriving at the campground, I find a campsite with an impressive view across Lost Lake Slough to East Beckwith Peak, making it an excellent location for a week of contemplation and mountain exploration.

Lost Lake Slough and East Beckwith Peak

After setting up camp I walk the Three Lakes Trail, a popular three-mile loop from the campground, climbing about 1000 feet to Lost Lake, Dollar Lake, and the Lost Lake waterfall. I am able to see East Beckwith Peak from many angles, so I can study it for a route to the summit. There is a crude trail at the west end of Lost Lake that seems to lead up to the cirque below the peaks. I mark it on my GPS so I can find it tomorrow when I attempt to summit the mountain. Back to camp now to settle in, organize my gear, and sit zazen.

Lost Lake

Waterfall into Lost Lake

Later

I'm gazing up at East Beckwith Peak, warm and golden in the evening sun. Can I make the steep climb to 12,400 feet tomorrow, probably most of it off trail? I know I have to try. My spirit longs to be up on the mountaintop. Will my aging body cooperate? Will the weather cooperate? According to Dennis, the campground host, it has rained each of the past five days, often quite heavily. I am lucky to have had a day with no rain to set up camp and do a little initial exploration.

Staying in a campground is one more concession to aging. For many years I backpacked, traveling deep into the wilderness and sleeping wherever I could find a location for my tiny tent. When carrying forty or fifty pounds on my back became too arduous I could drive my truck up some four-wheel-drive road and camp anywhere that I could find a level place to park. At seventy-seven I've come to depend on the amenities and conveniences of a campground.

Tuesday

I'm up early, hoping to summit East Beckwith Peak today. As I begin climbing on the trail I found the day before yesterday I encounter no real difficulties. Although the terrain is steep, the spruce/fir forest is open, with little deadfall. I had planned a route that would take me up the north ridge to the peak, so I keep moving in that direction as I climb through the trees.

After some time the forest ends abruptly and ahead of me exposed rocks stretch in talus slopes and boulder fields. Crossing such terrain is slow, exhausting, and dangerous. It requires hopping from rock to rock, with leg-breaking spaces in between and huge stones that I expect to be stable shifting suddenly under my weight. It's good practice though, demanding what Dogen Zenji calls "fully engaging body and mind," just to avoid injury.

Talus slope

Under a blazing sun, I step and leap across this rocky terrain for perhaps an hour, only to arrive at a sheer rock face blocking my way. I am now at about 11,200 feet, so still 1,200 vertical feet below the summit. To continue up I would have to descend, in order to circumvent this impasse, and then begin climbing once more. I am too tired to attempt that, so I make my way over yet another talus slope to a small patch of forest near timberline.

Once in the forest I can see that I would not have been able to ascend the north ridge to the summit. There is one place where rock spires and knife edges offer no footing. I can also see that ascent up the east ridge, although very steep, is probably workable, and the forest extends almost to that ridge. If the weather holds I may have another opportunity to climb to the peak.

North Ridge

Marcellina Mountain

When I am climbing I always hope to reach a summit, and just to be up above the trees, in alpine meadows, with spectacular views of mountain ranges as far as the eye can see, opens me to a profound and ineffable joy. Tired and happy, I make my way down through dwarf spruce forests and meadows blooming with alpine sunflowers, the twisted white blossoms of lousewort, and vivid pink paintbrush, an intense color that common flower only seems to attain at these altitudes. I eat lunch resting against a sun-warmed boulder, then lie down in the meadow and fall asleep for a quarter hour.

Paintbrush

Descending the mountain, the terrain becomes much steeper. As I near Lost Lake I suddenly feel dizzy, hot, and nauseated. I sit down to recover and a moment later throw up my lunch. I have reached some limit of exhaustion, my body simply refuses to go on, and my systems need to recalibrate.

How much to acquiesce to the limitations imposed by aging and how much to push against them? Don Juan, as presented in Carlos Castaneda's books about that shaman, lists four enemies of "The Man of Knowledge": Clarity, Power, Wisdom, and Old Age. Each of the first three is a hard-won accomplishment that once attained must be relinquished, defeated in Don Juan's model, or further attainments will not be realized. The last enemy, Old Age, is never vanquished, only held off as long as possible.

I approach Lost Lake down along the stream that feeds it, toward the waterfall that can be viewed from the Three Lakes trail, and discover another, even more beautiful waterfall above that one. I find a crude trail along the upper waterfall that is so steep that I must descend some of it on my butt, braking my descent with extended feet. That trail leads me to the Three Lakes Trail and back to my campsite, exhausted and fulfilled. I make dinner, sit zazen, and crawl contentedly into my sleeping bag. If the weather offers the opportunity, and if I have the energy to try again to ascend the mountain, I think the best route would begin on the south side of Lost Lake, then up through forest and meadow, to the east ridge of the peak.

Upper waterfall

Wednesday

Except for a brief shower yesterday evening, I've had two days without rain, and today looks like it could be another. After yesterday's exhausting hike I think I'll spend the day in camp, sitting zazen.

Later

Coming out of my tent after zazen there are dark clouds and thunder in the north and east, and there on the picnic table a dinner of pot roast, potatoes, and carrots! I've had only the briefest of conversations with the campground hosts, Connie and Dennis, and they seem to have taken a liking to me, perhaps because I'm staying for a full week. I received the same sort of attention from Ranger Rick at Capitol Reef when he learned that I planned to stay for a week. The people who work at these campgrounds seem to develop a very personal attachment, as if the place were their own, and they are delighted when someone wants to spend a week instead of the usual day or two.

There's a doe a few feet away as I write these notes, flicking her ears and munching fireweed. Probably the same one I saw last night. She seems unafraid, even though she must be aware of me. The sky has begun to clear and the thunder has ceased. I think, if the day dawns clear, I'll make another attempt to summit East Beckwith now that I believe I know the best route.

Strong wind again tonight. I am disturbed by this wind, made uneasy. This feels like a primal, not a reasonable reaction, since each night there has been this wind and each day has dawned calm and clear. Perhaps evolution selected for members of the species who took warning from wind. I'll read some Dogen, then sleep.

Thursday

It is a lovely morning, calm and clear. I would consider it a triumph to summit East Beckwith, or even to reach what's called the Horseshoe, just below the final pitch. The weather is changeable up here and I may not get another opportunity.

Setting out from camp at eight am I head up Three Lakes Trail to Lost Lake. From my experience the day before yesterday, and from studying the map, I decide that the best place to start up through the forest is on the south side of Lost Lake. I follow the path around the lake to a place clear of trees and start up. To my surprise I find a trail. It is steep and crude, but it takes me up through the forest for a mile or so, then fades out. By this time the forest is reduced to patches and I am high enough that I can see my route ahead. I continue on up, doing my best to avoid boulder fields and talus slopes by traveling through the patches of forest. I still have to cross some boulder fields, but that can be an enjoyable challenge when they don't go on for a half-mile and more, as was the case on my last attempt to summit.

Finally I climb up onto a knob with a few twisted and stunted spruces at about 11,500 feet. I can see what looks like a workable route up the east ridge and from there to the summit, but I have been climbing for over three hours now and I do not have the energy to go further. Of course I feel some regret not being able to make it to the summit, and as I've mentioned before just to be up in this alpine terrain above treeline, in boulder strewn meadows ablaze with wildflowers, and with views of mountain ranges as far as I can see, fills me with joy.

Knob with spruces

The wildflowers here in mid-July are at their splendid peak. Buttercups, paintbrush, asters, lousewort, alpine sunflowers, and blue columbine fill the meadows. The snowmelt still feeds small streams, creating tiny marshes where larkspur, elephant head, fireweed and cow parsnip are abundant. It has always intrigued me that species that grow both in alpine meadows and down lower, like paintbrush and Franciscan bluebells, are so much more intensely colored in their alpine setting.

Asters

I eat lunch in a small patch of forest, sleep for about fifteen minutes against a sun-warmed boulder, and make my way back to camp. Once in camp, I strip to shorts, walk down to the lake, and splash the cold lake water over my sweaty body.

Coming down the trail from Lost Lake I met Dennis, who asked if he could bring me dinner again tonight. My guess is that politically and culturally we have almost nothing in common, yet we seem to have made a strong connection through our love for this place. Later, appearing at my campsite, Dennis invites me to their trailer for dinner. I really would prefer to eat alone, and decide to accept. Dinner is pleasant enough, featuring trout that Dennis caught in the lake. My hunch about our differing social/political affinities is on target. I think we all sense this and the dinner conversation is entirely pleasant as we limit topics to hiking and camping. I leave shortly after dinner, hoping not to offend by telling them I like to spend the evening meditating.

It sprinkled before dinner, then rained heavily during our meal. Now, as the sun is setting, it's clear again. I'll sit zazen for an hour or two, then bed.

Friday

I'm not feeling very energetic today and I'm not sure why. Perhaps I'm not fully recovered from yesterday's strenuous hike. I think I'll hike to Beckwith Pass, three miles to the south and only 400 feet elevation gain. I hope to return off trail, where I experience the deepest intimacy with the land. On this warm, sunny day, the trail winds through spruce forests and meadows. I rest awhile at the pass, enjoying the impressive views to the east, then head cross-country, off-trail to Dollar Lake, the highest of the three lakes near the campground. I stay close to the base of the easternmost peak of the East Beckwith group, in order not to lose altitude.

Rock spires

For much of the time I follow a large animal trail across meadows filled with wildflowers, through spruce forests and willow thickets, and over talus slopes. No visible scat, so I don't know what animal created this trail. On the slopes of East Beckwith Mountain, close on my left, spires of rock alternate with steep meadows. Not far from Dollar Lake I can see possible routes of ascent to the summit of the easternmost peak of the East Beckwith Group, elevation 11,700 feet. If the weather holds while I'm here, perhaps I'll attempt to climb it.

Saturday

It rained a little before I got up and it's overcast this morning. A good morning for a hot breakfast, after which I'll spend the rest of it sitting zazen.

Gentle rain showers interspersed with sun all morning. Now I'm sitting under my shelter, after lunch, in a pounding thunderstorm. I'm stuck here for the duration of the storm and I have Dogen's essays to keep me company. For most of the retreat I have been reading the essay titled, "Body-and-Mind Study of the Way" (Shinjin Gakudo), which is just how I think of these solo retreats. I can consider zazen study with the mind and my long walks study with the body, and this distinction is arbitrary. Dogen says, "Now mountains, rivers, earth, the sun, the moon and stars are mind. At just this moment, what is it that appears directly in front of you?"

Heavy rain is directly in front of me just now, from which I must shelter myself. To take care of this body is study, to exhaust this body climbing mountains is study. "The body comes forth from the study of the way. Everything which comes forth from the study of the way is the true human body." To realize this, to experience this, to appreciate this is why I bring this body-mind to these mountains.

I'm sorry I didn't close the windows of my tent before this storm. I'm afraid the wind is blowing water into the tent. It rains heavily for a half hour or so, and when it lets up a bit I dash to the tent, where I find that, indeed, a significant amount of water has come in through one window. I'll mop up with towels and spend the rest of the afternoon on my cushion.

Sitting here in zazen, listening to the rain, I worry. When will it stop? Is all my gear staying dry? How will I prepare my next meal if it is still raining when that time comes? I'm sure that these concerns have an evolutionary basis. I imagine that those individuals who did not worry about the future did not pass on their genes. Sitting here in meditation, I don't try to stop worrying, I just surrender the worry, like all other thoughts and feelings, to breathing. Breathing is not something I do, as if I had some choice, it is something in which I participate. In order to breathe I need oxygen, which means I need to be on earth, with green plants growing. For these plants to grow water, soil, and sunlight are necessary; the earth needs to be at a precise distance from the sun. If I am thorough in this analysis, I will see that the entire universe is breathing and that all of it, incessantly changing is my True Nature. From this perspective it doesn't matter if my gear stays dry or how I eat. Whatever happens is simply opportunity for practice. Surrendering all concerns to breathing, I rest in my True Nature.

The rain goes on, sometimes light, sometimes heavy, until 7:30 pm. I make dinner from the lunch I had prepared for the hike I planned for tomorrow and eat it in the truck. I'll sit again before sleep and probably leave for home tomorrow morning.

Sunday

This morning is much like yesterday, heavy with moisture, with some clouds already in the sky. Time to go.

Later

On the high plains somewhere north of Ojo Caliente, sunlight falling between magnificent cumulus clouds dapples the hills and mesas with patterns of light and shadow. I have Beethoven's Ninth Symphony on the truck stereo and when The Ode to Joy rings out it seems to perfectly express my happiness and my gratitude for this week alone in the mountains.

The Path is the Goal
(Truchas Peak)

The mountains, rivers, grasses, trees, and forests are always emanating a subtle, precious light, day and night, always emanating a subtle, precious sound, demonstrating and expounding to all people the unsurpassed ultimate truth.
—Yuan-sou

The hike to North Truchas Peak, up the North Fork of the Rio Quemado, is long and arduous. It begins with ten miles on a bone jarring four-wheel drive road out of Truchas, a tiny mountain village thirty miles northeast of Santa Fe, in the Sangre de Cristo Mountains. The trail begins at about nine thousand feet, winds seven or eight miles up the Rio Quemado, then switchbacks up a steep slope that opens onto a cirque surrounded on three sides by the five Truchas Peaks. From here an even steeper and almost imperceptible trail ascends a talus slope to North Truchas summit, at just over thirteen thousand feet.

Jim Kando Green and I have attempted this climb every summer for several years. Sometimes we make it to the summit and sometimes we don't. We have been driven back down by strong winds, threatening to blow us off the ridge below the summit, and by the fierce electrical storms that the mountains generate on summer afternoons. This particular August morning begins clear and bright.

After several hours we reach the cirque below the summits, where we stop to rest after the effort of the climb from the trailhead, before marshaling our energy for the even more strenuous climb to the top. Here house-size boulders that have tumbled down from the peaks rest in a mosaic of small forests and meadows. In late summer gentian, alpine buttercup, moss campion and other high mountain wildflowers are abundant. Several clear streams thread through this landscape, gathering at the lip of the cirque in a delicate waterfall that becomes the Rio Quemado, Spanish for Burned River. No one seems to know how this mountain stream acquired its name.

Cirque below the peaks

  I climb up on a boulder to scan the mountainside for the faint trail that leads to the ridge below the summit, and spot a bear turning over rocks on the talus slope above us. Strange to see a forest creature out beyond the reach of trees, but at this time of year a species of moth comes here in great numbers to lay eggs beneath the rocks of this barren slope, a fine meal for our omnivorous friend.

  Cumulus clouds have formed by this time, and we can see a thunderstorm building to the northeast. As we start up the talus slope, I say to Jim, "As soon as we hear thunder, we're turning back."

  "Absolutely," he responds, knowing the danger posed by electrical storms on open slopes.

Thunderstorm over North Truchas Peak

    Wanting to reach the summit, we ignore our sensible decision. As the storm grows in size and proximity, and we can hear the first rumbles of distant thunder, we reassess the situation, promising ourselves that if it doesn't pass to the north we will retreat in plenty of time to seek shelter in the cirque below. The first big drops of rain clearly demonstrate the extent of our denial. Within a few minutes we are being lashed by wind-driven rain and hail. Deafening claps of thunder follow lightning without pause as we leap from rock to rock down the talus slope, finally taking shelter in the overhang of a huge boulder. As the storm rages, Jim takes out his backpack stove and prepares tea. We sit in this refuge from nature's cauldron, drinking our tea in silence, awed by the power of the storm. When then lightning seems to have passed on to the next drainage, we pack up and head back down. The rain continues on and off all the way down the trail and we reach the truck wet, exhausted, and supremely happy.

Although we fail to make the summit, I have learned on these adventures that reaching a predetermined goal is of little importance. Several years ago I was climbing a ridge in the San Juan Mountains of Colorado, hoping to reach a twelve thousand foot crest. There was no trail, and the going was much more difficult than I had imagined. I stopped at about 10,000 feet, in the midst of an extraordinary arrangement of immense, angular granite boulders, from where I could look for miles to the valley below and the peaks beyond. Lying back on a rock, feeling frustrated by how little progress I had made and realizing that I would now have to start back, I gazed up at the sky to see an eagle soaring effortlessly down the ridge. While I lay there admiring the great bird, it uttered a piercing cry and I was sure it had come to tell me, "Musai, stop complaining. The beauty all around you is completely sufficient."

There have been other times when we do reach the summit. There the granite substrate, exposed where all vegetation and soil have been scoured away by wind and rain, is revealed as large multihued crystals, each one a jewel.

Truchas Peak from the ridge between Truchas and North Truchas Peaks

Looking down we can see Truchas Lakes below us to the east and the view is spectacular in all directions. This is my magic mountain.

Truchas Lakes

I Am This Beauty
(Sangre de Cristo Mountains, Colorado)

I have always known that at last I would take this road, but yesterday I did not know it would be today.
—Narihara

Thursday

There are at least two of us setting off on my 73rd birthday for another solo retreat in the mountains. There is the thoughtful, even cautious adult, who has prepared carefully, with appropriate containers for gear and food, and comprehensive lists, to make sure we are well equipped and that nothing is forgotten. Then there is a ten-year-old boy—excited, enthusiastic, ready for adventure. They travel well together and make a good team.

Friday

A difficult night. Restless dreams having to do with not deserving this time alone. I should be serving others in some way, I am selfish to take this time alone. Certainly I reject this consciously. I have come to believe that these trips are crucial to my sense of well-being. I am convinced that clarity of mind, depth of practice, capacity to serve, and a general sense that this world I have created is good are all enhanced by this week alone in the mountains.

One very enjoyable aspect of a trip like this is that I can do what I want, when I want. I am freed from any imposed schedule and from considering what others want to do and when.

A two-hour walk after lunch, up canyon, off trail, along the stream, then back above the stream, where the canyon wall slopes steeply away. Just wandering, very slowly, acquainting myself with this place. I love hiking this way—meandering off trail, stopping often, sometimes on terrain where I need to place each foot carefully, greeted by flowers, rock outcrops, and trees that no one else ever encounters. As Wang-wei says in one of his poems, "Wonderful things that only I know."

Ancient juniper

Massive, incredibly gnarled junipers on this south-facing slope. How long have they held to this rocky hillside?

Saturday

I set out with a plan to climb Pyramid Mountain or Venable Peak, but clouds are rolling in on the trail up to Three Forks and I consider changing my plan, since I certainly don't want to be on alpine slopes if thunderstorms seem at all likely. By the time I reach Three Forks the sky is blue again, so I head up the North Fork trail toward the peaks. This trail is clearly not much used. In some places grass grows on the trail, at other places I have to push through willows.

I arrive at a point where I have to decide whether to climb up Pyramid Mountain to the west or Venable Peak to the east. I decide on Venable, since I am doubtful that I can make it to the top of either, and if I can get up to twelve thousand feet on the slopes of Venable, I can traverse over to the Middle Fork drainage and come down through new territory.

    Climbing up from eleven thousand feet, I am soon above timberline. Walking off trail on steep slopes demands complete mindfulness. My mind is emptied of any consideration other than where to place the next foot, and when I stop to gaze around, as I frequently do, the grandeur of the place, or the fascinating details of some rock or alpine flower so fill my consciousness that all other thoughts are obliterated. The necessity for mindfulness is even more critical coming down. Going up, if I stumble, I will likely fall into the hill. Going down, a stumble can lead to a bone-cracking tumble down a rocky slope.

    I am always ecstatic up here. I can remember that joy to some extent at any time, but when I am here I am always astonished by its magnitude.

    Clouds again begin to fill the sky, so at twelve thousand feet it seems prudent to start down. I travel down along a spine of rock, sometimes one side, sometimes the other, sometimes on top. No rain after all, so back to camp and a quick, cold bath in the creek before dinner and zazen.

Pissing by Moonlight

Need to piss.
Snug in my bag,
my sleepwarm body says no.
Need to piss wins out.
Standing there naked,
a swath of ground
silvered by moonlight,
I look up to see
the moon,
just emerging over the edge of the cliff.
Sting of cold night air on my skin,
core still dreamily warm,
I stand for minutes
to watch the gibbous moon
sail free of the cliff,
silhouetting a ponderosa.
Deep gratitude
returning to my nest.

Sunday

South Crestone Lake is my destination today. From the trailhead, the trail switchbacks up through conifer and aspen forests, across high meadows blooming with swaths of golden pea. Coming out of the forest, magnificent granite shoulders and spires come into view. They loom above me as I make my way over the final steep pitch, across talus and boulders to the lake. South Crestone is a classic alpine lake, surrounded by granite outcrops and stunted pines. It sits beneath the 14,000' grandeur of Mount Adams.

I enjoy my lunch in sunlight and watch an eagle circle over the lake, then climb on a thermal to soar over Mount Adams in just a matter of minutes. What a contrast to my laborious ascent of these mountains. Clouds blow in, the wind is chill, time to pack up and head back down the trail.

Monday

Zazen as refuge. What I like and dislike about myself are ephemeral manifestations. Zazen reveals who I am, and that is vast beyond imagining. Nothing to change, nothing to prefer. Something/nothing unfolding into everything.

Only when I'm sitting zazen am I not trying, in one way or another, to arrange the world to better suit myself. Most of the time I am embarked on a program of self-improvement, which suits my inner critic, or I am trying to increase my level of contentment, or I am attempting to serve others in ways that I think will improve their lives, or I am trying to arrange the world and its inhabitants toward an end that I think will be some sort of improvement over the status quo. In all of these pursuits, of course, I am often frustrated. Yet I persist, and why not? They are honorable pursuits. Zazen releases me.

Waterfall

Tuesday

I lose the trail just below the escarpment that holds back Willow Lake. When I get to the rockface I can see slopes and cracks that I can probably use to make my way up to the top. I make my way across a rock ledge, cross the creek beneath the waterfall coming down from the lake, clamber up a steep, forested slope, and again find the trail.

Mountain streams leap and plunge.
Gleaming in sunlight,
they splash and tumble
to the plain.

Subterranean water
is without drama.
Flowing slowly, imperceptibly,
All life is its expression.

Don't seek some special state
in zazen.
Even if you find it—
a stagnant pool.
Just let go of all stories,
it's only your stories
that sustain the illusion of self.
Old Joshu knew:
"Like a ball tossed on rushing water."

The mountains and streams and weather patterns don't care at all about my welfare, or concern themselves with what I want. I have to adapt to them. I do so willingly and without complaint; I am happy here. After an afternoon of zazen, each tree and rock is vivid, marvelous. Dinner now, then more zazen.

Wednesday

I start up along the North Fork trail, enjoying how the terrain changes as I gain altitude. The trees become smaller and the forests less dense. Broad, sloping meadows, nearly devoid of trees begin to appear. Massive rocky outcrops are all around me, the bones of the mountain pushing through. I stop in a stand of small aspens to drink in this beauty. Across a narrow valley a steep meadow dotted with wildflowers rises up to the peaks, the scattered trees there now mostly weathered snags.

All at once I know I am this beauty. I am suffused with an emotion that I cannot name or describe. It is so intense that I bury my face in my hands and begin to weep. The weeping progresses to sobbing, then to bawling, and then I am laughing and crying at the same time. There is no place, no me, just an ineffable sense of beauty, harmony, joy.

I don't know how long this goes on, perhaps only two or three minutes. Then all the emotion drains away and I return to a *sense of self.* Feeling a profound *sense* of peace and well being, I continue on my journey. I do not take any photos for several hours because everything I see, large and small, is extraordinarily beautiful and perfect. I cannot choose.

I am this beauty

Stopping on a mountain trail
to appreciate the beauty.
I am this beauty.
Place and self dissolve
into laughing, crying,
only beauty, harmony, joy remain.
Silence then,
and unsurpassed peace.
Walking on,
every rock and tree
lit from within.

On my way back, walking along the trail in a reverie, I am startled to a halt by the piercing cry of a marmot. I know from the sound that the animal must be close. "Nice to have you here," I say, "would you mind revealing yourself?" I look all around and can see no one. "I guess you would," I say, "nice to know you're so close, anyway."

I haven't gone more than a few steps when I see below me, perched on a rock, a handsome marmot. He can't be more than 30 feet away. I carefully put down my hiking stick and get out my camera. The marmot sits perfectly still while I take several shots, and when I bend down to pick up my stick, he flows down over the rock into hiding.

Today I was out for eleven hours, climbing four thousand feet in the course of the hike. I misread the map and the territory, missed the off trail route to Groundhog Basin, and walked almost all the way to the pass over to San Isabel Lake. I believe that the hard work of hiking off trail at altitude has a lot to do with the delight I experience up here. I resist associating effort with joy. I want my effort to pay off big—a little effort for a lot of joy. But it doesn't seem to work that way. What I attain with little effort is something much thinner than joy—pleasure, at best. When I avoid effort my life feels empty, unsatisfying.

Thursday

A quiet day. A day in camp. A day of zazen. I am so easily entertained out here. The play of shadows on the roof of my tent, as sunlight filters through leaves moved by a breeze. Tomorrow I return home, with some regret at leaving this solitude. So many of the supports for a sense of self are missing out here. No work, no relationships, no entertainment. Life reduced to basics opens to deep feeling and deep samadhi. Emotions arise and pass away, both stronger and more ephemeral than when I am immersed in my usual life. Joy and sorrow and all the lesser manifestations of those emotions visit me for awhile and vanish, coming and going like the light and the dark, the sun and the rain. I think almost not at all out here about world events or financial concerns, only occasionally about my therapy clients and Zen students, and not much about those dearest to me.

A cup of coffee in the shade as I write these notes, then a very quick, very cold bath in the stream, and more zazen. Looking up at the sky, a storm of cotton carried on the breeze from the cottonwoods lower down. How extravagant nature is. What infinitesimal fraction of this storm of tiny seeds will germinate into trees? Up here, none, yet some float down here and many more are carried to still higher elevations. What a marvelous dance.

Saturday

Departure day. I need to acknowledge that the transition back to my life at home is enormous. I have lived day-to-day, moment-to-moment, for over a week. Now it's back to planning and to negotiating almost all aspects of my life with numerous other beings.

Brief Encounter On The Way Home

Descending the mountain,
early morning light,
a pronghorn bounds across the road.
I stop.
He stops.
We gaze awhile at each other
then each turns to where his heart calls.

Autumn

Lessons in Impermanence
(Bandelier National Monument)

> *Chosha went roaming the mountains one day. On returning, when he came to the gate the congregation leader said, "Where have you been, Master?"*
> *Chosha said, "Roaming the mountains."*
> *The congregation leader said, "Where did you go?"*
> *Chosha said, "First I followed the fragrant gasses on the way out, then I came back pursuing the falling flowers."*
> —Secrets Of The Blue Cliff Record, case 36.
> Translated by Thomas Cleary, Shambhala Publications, 2000.

One of my favorite autumn hikes in Bandelier takes me up along Mesa del Rito for about five miles, then down into Alamo Canyon, one of the many canyons carved into the soft, volcanic rock of the Monument. There is no official trail here, but of course the large mammals—deer, elk, bear, and cougar—create trails throughout the wilderness, and especially along watercourses. I follow their tracks for another five or six miles, down the stream that flows in all but the driest months, enjoying the magnificent autumn foliage.

Aspens display their golden leaves in the upper sections, giving way to gambel oak further downstream, offering a spectrum of colors from rust to copper to gold. The sculpted rock formations here have been created over millennia when harder layers of volcanic rock and random boulders form capstones, while the underlying tuff is eroded by wind, rain, and snow. Wandering down through this earth womb I meet the well-worn trail that crosses the canyon on its way to the ancient sculpture of the Stone Lions. I have a steep climb of several hundred vertical feet before crossing the mesa and descending back to the trailhead in Frijoles Canyon.

Alamo Canyon

The entire Pajarito Plateau, where Bandelier is situated, was formed from volcanic eruptions over a period from 13 million to one million years ago. In his book, *The Mountains of New Mexico*, Robert Julyan describes this process as a "geological drama [that] had a dual climax 1.6 and 1.22 million years ago with two cataclysmic explosions from a huge magma chamber. Vast quantities of ash and debris blanketed the area, settling and coalescing into distinctive, easily eroded tuff deposits."[1]

Waterfall

The path of water

The mountains that exploded during these eruptions were as high as the Himalayas, and the immense plateau of volcanic rock left behind has been eroded into a complex landscape of canyons, mesas, waterfalls, and sculpted volcanic tuff formations. The Monument is famous for its Anasazi ruins, Anasazi being the name given by anthropologists to a people that lived here perhaps as long ago as 1500 BCE. This hunter/gatherer/agrarian people carved their homes in the soft volcanic rock and these cliff dwellings, which still exist today, are easily reached from the visitor center on asphalt paths. Beyond this busy hub are miles of backcountry wilderness where I can wander in solitude, and while I consider it too hot in summer to enjoy hiking here, when I would rather be high in the *Sangre de Cristo Mountains*, autumn, winter, and spring offer abundant opportunities to wander through this unique wilderness.

Ponderosa in snow

August 2011

   A deep sadness underlies my account of hiking here. In July of this year a tree downed by wind fell across a power line, sparking the biggest wildfire in New Mexico's history. The Las Conchas fire burned for weeks, extending far down into Bandelier's canyons. In late August thunderstorms drenched the Jemez Mountains and the Pajarito Plateau. Falling on unstable soils, stripped of so much living vegetation, these storms washed debris from the fire, including charred trees as much three feet in diameter, far downstream. Mud, too, came down with the storms, so that now my beloved canyons are choked with piles of debris on top of a thick layer of muck. As a hiker friend of mine remarked, "We won't see Bandelier recover in our lifetime."

   Although I am saddened by this, I know that when I venture again down into the canyons in a year, two years, five years, I will see abundant displays of wildflowers, young aspen saplings sprouting from the root systems that survived the fire, willows and cottonwoods emerging along the streams, and juniper, pinon pine, and ponderosa pine establishing new forests in their respective niches. In his first teaching, the Buddha asserted that impermanence is the fundamental nature of manifest existence and warned against attachment and aversion. All that arises is subject to decay, and endless transformation is an immutable law. Dogen Zenji reminds us, "...simply, flowers fall amid our longing, and weeds spring up amid our antipathy."[2]

1. *The Mountains of New Mexico*, Robert Julyan, University of New Mexico Press, 2006 p.76
2. *Moon in a Dewdrop*, ed. Kazuaki Tanahashi, North Point Press, 1985 p.69.

Autumn in the Desert
(Capitol Reef National Park)

Traveler, there is no path. You make your path as you travel.
—Antonio Machado

Friday

I meet Rick Stinchman, retired academic, volunteer ranger, and author of *Capitol Reef National Park, The Complete Hiking and Touring Guide*, behind the desk at the Capitol Reef Visitor Center. Rick spends three months each year at Capitol Reef, guiding and advising visitors and wandering the backcountry. When I tell him I will be here for a week he is surprised and delighted. Most people, he tells me, spend one or two days, on their way to more popular destinations. I like to get into a place, I comment, and that connects us at once. He waxes enthusiastic about the best places to hike in the park and I buy his book.

Setting up camp at Cedar Mesa, a primitive campsite about 30 miles South of the Visitor Center, I make a disappointing discovery: I did not pack my tent. I sleep in the camper shell on the back of my truck, but my tent is my zendo, where I take shelter to meditate, so I will miss it. I can manage if it doesn't rain and none is predicted. I have plenty of warm clothing for early morning and late evening zazen. The Buddha attained great enlightenment under a tree so who can say what opportunities await me while meditating beneath a juniper.

Saturday

I am up by six am, boil water for tea, eat some trailmix, and make an early start for Upper Muley Twist Canyon. Maneuvering on the challenging four-wheel drive road leading to the trailhead, I back into a boulder, tear off a mudguard, and dent a fender. These jeep trails are hard on vehicles and I am grateful for my little truck that takes me to places I would never be able to access otherwise.

Muley Arch

Wandering all day through the sculpted sandstone of the canyon, arriving back at my truck after seven pm, I see no reason to travel back over that difficult road this evening. I think I'll make dinner, sit a couple of periods of zazen and spend the night here at the trailhead.

9 pm

I'm watching the moon rise over the canyon wall after an hour or so of zazen under a juniper. Until the moon appeared, the darkness was profound. During zazen, a light breeze, the sound of desert insects, and once a bat flew close enough for me to feel the air from its wings on my face.

I have the clear and certain knowledge that I am creating this place. Images, emotions, thoughts arise and pass away. I become the ancient rocks, then I imagine a mountain lion hovering nearby and frighten myself. Surrendering all to breathing I think of Siddhartha Gautama, soon to realize himself as the Buddha, assailed by Mara, the Lord of Death, as he sat in deep samadhi under the Bodhi Tree. Mara brought in everything he could to confuse and distract Siddhartha—images and ideas to evoke fear, anger, resentment and desire. Through it all, Siddhartha just sat, to discover that only these thoughts and emotions separated him from his True Nature and *annutara samyak sambodhi*, complete, perfect enlightenment. I'll spend the night here.

Sunday

I rise at dawn, put on my parka and warm hat to ward of the cold, and head up the trail to the Strike Valley overlook. Sitting here on the ridge, far above the Strike Valley, watching the sun rise over the sandstone formations of the canyon wall, I lack nothing and know deep contentment.

Breakfast over, I'll drive back to camp, prepare a lunch, and set off to hike up Sheet's Gulch, where I expect to find some impressive slots and narrows. I have been warned that I might have to wade through some stretches.

Setting out from the trailhead around noon, I walk for a mile or two up a broad wash. Full sunlight, except where I can pause under a cottonwood. Mornings and evenings are cool, and the sun, for a few hours after 11 am, is punishing. I'm glad to be here in late September. In summer, with much higher temperatures and the sun near the zenith, the heat would be intolerable.

Pools in Sheet's Gulch narrows

Soon the canyon narrows and I come to thirty or forty yards of pools that I have to wade. Walking knee and sometimes thigh deep through thick red water and viscous mud feels like an initiation, allowing me access to the sinuous narrows ahead

Narrows

In some places I can touch both sides of the canyon at once, the walls fluted and sculpted into flowing shapes. In one narrow section I have to make my way over and under chockstones, refrigerator size boulders rolled down canyon during flash floods and jammed into especially narrow places. These huge rocks are carried by a soup of water, mud, gravel and stones, downed and uprooted trees. The narrows are extremely dangerous during the summer storm season. Any thing here when this wall of slurry comes through is carried along until everything that doesn't get stuck in the twists and turns of the canyon is deposited on the alluvial fan at the mouth of the canyon. Coming out of the narrows, I look up to see a formation that reminds me of the Buddha's hand in the gesture of No Fear. A benediction.

It always takes a while to get used to the grit and sweat out here and I'm beginning to feel comfortable. Everything is wearing in holes on this abrasive landscape. I will need a new daypack, hiking pants, leather gloves.

Monday 6:30 am

I'm writing these notes while still in bed. This is the middle day of my retreat. It seems more difficult this year and I'm not sure why. No tent, hurting my foot on the Upper Muley Twist hike, the desert heat compared to the coolness of the mountains, less daylight than in summer? All of these perhaps, and although I would like to deny it, just being older probably plays a part. I have a tendency to deny aging—not so bad an adjustment, I think.

Later

I'm sitting beneath a cottonwood along Pleasant Creek. I broke camp early and decided on a short hike to Cassady Arch, before heading into Torrey for ice and gas, then out to Cathedral Campground. It didn't work out as planned. I headed off for the arch at 10:30 am for a three and one half mile round trip. I was sure I could be back for lunch, so I took only my small water bottle. I ascended about 1000 feet in one mile over a good trail, and came to a trail junction clearly marked with a sign: ".5 miles to Cassady Arch." I took the wrong trail and after a half hour of downhill walking the trail ran out and no sign of the arch.

Fern's Nipple

Getting lost, however, has its own rewards. I saw the formation known as Fern's Nipple and was able to photograph it through a window formed by an ancient juniper snag.

By noon and I was hungry and I knew I must have gone more than one half mile, so I started back. When I got to the trail junction I saw my mistake and realized that I had probably descended most of the 1000 feet before starting back. I arrived at the truck hungry, tired, very thirsty, and with another injury, this time to my other foot.

I've also come down with a cold, which along with two foot injuries and no tent has made this a difficult retreat. Yet I am happy here, happy to be alone in this magnificent place, alone in my zazen, alone with my thoughts and feelings. With no one else to consider, I set my own schedule and go my own way. I make my own path as I travel.

Tuesday 7:00 am

I'm enjoying cup of tea after sitting this morning. During zazen I realized that through all the difficulties and disappointments of this trip I don't feel that I am wrong or deficient. This rather amazes me. A result of Zen practice, or simply of aging? Whatever the reason, it is a great blessing.

Some people I know seem never to have been troubled by feelings of deficiency, but this theme, that I should be different, that a better person would make better choices, has been with me all my life. I feel tender toward that struggling part of me and glad to know that he can be less prominent in my life.

A chill wind this morning. If it continues I will feel the absence of a tent keenly. Until now, except for gentle breezes during the day, it has been quite still, especially mornings and evenings.

Later

I'm glad I tried the Cassady Arch hike again. It actually is the easy hike I anticipated—less than two hours out and back. The trail takes me to a rise from where I can look down into the arch and from there I can walk out on top of it.

I have lunch under a fruit tree in the idyllic campground at Fruita. Mormon settlers, coaxing abundance from the hard desert country, created this oasis of fruit trees along the Fremont River. After lunch I take the Cathedral loop, a four- wheel drive road of fifty miles or so, up into the desert country North of Hiway 24. This is dry, dry land—sandstone towers and ridges, with only a few scattered junipers and desert shrubs. I stop at several overlooks. Starkly beautiful country that I hope to walk through tomorrow.

Cassady Arch

Wednesday

I wake while it is still dark, have breakfast, and break camp by moonlight and dawnlight. Doing these simple chores, I am reminded how any activity can be a meditation. All that's required is mindfulness, and perhaps love. If love seems too extravagant a word, then respect.

Shortly after sunrise I set off to hike in the South Desert out to Temple Rock. The early morning sun creates sharp contrasts of light and shadow among the dramatic formations of the desert. I thought it would be awfully hot walking back from Temple Rock, but although the sun blazes as usual, the air temperature is probably no higher than 80 degrees and there is a fresh breeze. The solitude and the silence are complete. Life is not abundant out here. At some point I realize I have seen no ravens and no buzzards. They know where to find their meals--depending on death, they depend on life.

Formations in South Desert

Later

The trail into Cohab Canyon begins at the scenic drive along the Fremont River, switchbacks up a steep slope of red earth and black boulders to a sheer sandstone cliff, runs along the base of the cliff for 100 yards or so, until a narrow slot opens into the Canyon.

Every canyon in this twisted landscape is unique, and this one is surprisingly verdant, with grasses, shrubs, and many large, healthy pinon pines. There are narrow side canyons, going back only a short distance before ending at sheer sandstone walls. I explore three, each quite different in its contours and vegetation.

Side canyon

Before turning back, I climb out of the canyon on a trail leading to an overlook of Fruita. Below me sits lush, green Fruita, the Fremont River glinting in the evening sun, and barren, multicolored cliffs on both sides.

Thursday

The Campground at Fruita is lovely, but I value my privacy and solitude and prefer more remote locations. I break camp by moonlight, as quietly as I can, in order not to disturb other campers.

From the Fruita campground, I drive down a dirt road to Panorama Point. I'll make a cup of tea here and watch the sunrise from the cab of my truck, since there is a chill wind this morning. After breakfast here on the point, I'll begin my journey homeward, visiting Natural Bridges National Monument on my way back home.

Friday

I walk down into the canyon of Natural Bridges National Monument on a marvelously engineered trail, with stone steps and rustic ladders. The quality of workmanship makes me think it was probably done by the Civilian Conservation Corps, that agency created by FDR to give work to the unemployed during the Great Depression. Wherever I encounter the efforts of these men and women, usually in National Parks and Monuments, I am impressed by the elegance and durability of their work.

I walk under two of the three bridges, up another finely engineered trail out of the canyon, and across the mesa back to my truck. I talk to things out here, just as I used to do as a child, granting sentience and intention to the components of the landscape. I talk to the trees and the moon, to animals and insects. Walking across the mesa, in the heat of the late afternoon sun, I ask the breeze if she would please grace me with her cool breath. I'm delighted when she grants my request. I don't converse with the sun. I say good morning and good night, out of respect. The sun seems implacable.

I don't spend much time reading on these retreats, but I always bring at least one Buddhist book and one nature book. Reading Craig Childs', *The Secret Knowledge of Water*, I gained more respect for my journaling. I have sometimes thought my adventures compromised by writing about them, while Childs clearly sees his writing as an integral and important part of his journey. In describing an episode where he entered a cave through a waterfall, he is anguished as memory of that extraordinary experience fades while he is trying to reach his notebook.

Natural bridge

Winter

Disappointment and Redemption
(Plaza Blanca)

Above all, do not lose your desire to walk: every day I walk myself into a state of well-being and walk away from every illness. I have walked myself into my best thoughts, and I know of no thought so burdensome that one cannot walk away from it. Thus if one just keeps walking, everything will be all right.

—Soren Kierkegaard

December

It has been many years since I walked this loop in the Carson National Forest, near Abiquiu, NM. The route takes me up Cañon Madera to a remarkable white sandstone formation known locally as Plaza Blanca or The White Place, across broken country of hills and washes, and back down through a maze of arroyos and sculpted rock.

Cañon Madera marks the boundary of the Plaza Blanca Land Grant, a ten square mile chunk of territory chopped out of the Carson National Forest. The last time I walked here the difference between national forest and land grant amounted to a line on the map. This time, after hiking a mile or so, I come to a barbed wire fence with signs announcing, "Private Property, No Trespassing."

Knowing the canyon to be the national forest boundary, I find a way up the east wall and continue my journey across the low hills at the foot of Sierra Negra. After another mile I find myself looking down on a large ranch compound in the canyon, situated just below one of the impressive white sandstone formations that give the land grant its name. Although I can see no sign of human presence, I want to be sure to avoid any possible confrontation, so I continue walking above the canyon, on national forest terrain.

I love these hikes close to the solstice, when the sun is a low arc across the southern sky and the days are brief. No flowers or foliage, except the muted green of pinon pine needles and the gray green scales of juniper branches; the land all muted browns and grays, my footsteps crunching on patches of crystallized snow, glittering in sunlight. The air is so dry and clear that even the mountains on the horizon are clearly etched against the deep blue sky

With the detours dictated by new fences and development, I know I won't reach my intended destination, so I descend into the canyon a couple of miles past the ranch and up the west wall. I expect to walk across the land grant without hindrance, but, in fact, I encounter stables, a corral, and barbed wire fences. I know that the population of New Mexico is growing, and that development is inevitable, and I am always saddened to see human interventions on land where I once wandered freely.

After walking for a couple of hours, I climb a hill to get my bearings and can see, off in the distance, the maze of arroyos through which I will make my way back to the truck.

Gray sandstone

By the time I descend into this tangled array of arroyos the sun is low in the west, clouds have moved in, and I am tired. Trudging in the fading light through gray sandstone formations and patches of old snow suits my gloomy mood.

Sunlit tower

As I near my truck, the sun breaks through the overcast just before setting, bathing a sandstone tower in soft light and seeming to say, "Come back, find a new route, don't be discouraged."

January

After my failed attempt to reach Plaza Blanca last month, and my disappointment with development on the land grant, this is a redemptive hike. The setting sun on the previous hike had beckoned me back and on this walk I find my new route.

Brian is my companion this time and we begin our walk in near perfect winter hiking conditions—sunny, no breeze, temperature in the mid twenties. We park at the mouth of Cañon Madera and walk up canyon for a half mile or so, then climb up the east wall of the canyon, to be on public land.

We skirt a sandstone wall of turrets and battlements, looking for a route north, on the flank of Sierra Negra.

Twin towers

The terrain offers easy walking as we climb an earthen ramp that leads us up between two stone towers.

Looking down through the towers

We stop for a midmorning break and snack on a patch of level ground beyond the towers. I consult my map and tell Brian that we will need to eat lunch no later than twelve thirty, so we can start our return journey by one, in order to arrive back at the truck before dark. This means that, depending on the challenges we encounter, we might not reach our destination, the sandstone formations of Plaza Blanca.

Brian looks at me for a moment, then says, "This is beginning to look like aimless wandering."

"Exactly," I answer, "my preferred method of travel out here."

We continue on our way, down through canyons, up across mesas, north toward the west running ridge of Sierra Negra. Our destination lies beyond that ridge, northwest of the mountain.

The Pedernal

 We find a good route about a third of the way up the mountain, with expansive views across broken country of hills and arroyos, all the way to the Pedernal, that iconic Northern New Mexico landmark made famous in the twentieth century by Georgia O'Keeffe.

 After walking for five or six miles, we drop back down into Cañon Madera and before long come to Blacktop, a hill named for the black basalt cap that stabilizes the sandstone beneath. I know now we are close and will likely reach our destination. Just a few minutes before our deadline of twelve thirty, we top a hill and there is Plaza Blanca, directly before us.

 As we sit there in the windless, cloudy afternoon, contemplating the effects of time and weather on the ancient rock in front of us, I say to Brian, "Only one thing could make me any happier—a break in the clouds that would give me better light for a photo of those rocks." Less than five minutes pass before the sun breaks through, bathing Plaza Blanca in soft light.

Plaza Blanca

    After lunch we climb back up onto the western flank of Sierra Negra and make our way back by a different route. One of the advantages of hiking off trail is that even with an out and back trip I am never covering quite the same ground, experiencing quite the same terrain. I am always struck on these hikes by how little it matters which route I take, and by how many intriguing alternatives there are once I leave a trail. I also realize out here how little I need to be content: a vehicle to get me here, a good pair of boots, a good pack, sufficient clothing to keep me warm and dry, and sufficient food and water to sustain me. I like having a GPS and a camera, but I don't need them, just as I don't need so much of what this consumption deranged society tries to convince me is essential to my happiness.

    There is great variety in the rocks that litter the ground here. Sandstone from prehistoric seabeds predominates, and there is black, volcanic basalt, dazzling white quartz, and granite with many colors wound together in fascinating patterns. Brian comments that one could spend an afternoon in one square yard of this country and never be bored.

We pass different sandstone formations on the way back, beckoning us into the mysteries of hidden canyons, but it is late, we are tired, and we continue on, knowing that there are inexhaustible opportunities for future exploration out here.

Sculpted sandstone

Late in the afternoon we drop down into yet another a canyon of intricately sculpted sandstone that we think will lead us back to Cañon Madera and our vehicle.

Sunset light

As we emerge from the canyon the sun sinks beneath the cloud cover, brilliantly illuminating pale sandstone formations against the shadowed backdrop of Sierra Negra.

The route we thought would lead us directly back to the truck instead leads to a jeep trail that we follow to the hard road, where we find ourselves a mile and a half from the truck. Exhausted after a long day navigating rugged terrain, we trudge the road back under a cloudy sky and reach the truck just before it becomes too dark to see.

The return route may have added distance to an already long hike, but it also confers a gift: a new trailhead that altogether avoids Cañon Madera and the private land of the Plaza Blanca Land Grant. What's more, it would be possible, at least in dry weather, to drive a mile or more on the jeep trail, thereby shortening two very long hikes, and affording further exploration of the upper reaches of Cañon Madera. I do not believe I have ever encountered a detour, difficulty, or disappointment while on one of these hikes that did not open new possibilities and lead to new delights.

Discovering Myself
(Syncline in the New Mexico Desert)

> *Do not be an embodier of fame; do not be a storehouse of schemes; do not be an undertaker of projects; do not be a proprietor of wisdom. Embody to the fullest what has no end and wander where there is no trail. Hold on to all that you have received from heaven, but do not think you have gotten anything. Be empty, that is all.*
>
> —Chuang tzu

I begin every hike with a gatha, a Buddhist term for a brief statement of intention, gratitude, or praise:

Today as I walk, I vow with all sentient beings, to honor this place and all who live here, and to discover myself.

In the sharp cold and brilliant sunlight of a New Mexico winter morning, I find myself chanting this gatha as I leave my truck to walk into the syncline just off Highway 550, northwest of Bernalillo, New Mexico. This trough like formation in sandstone bedrock, about four miles across, is bounded on the west by the escarpment of Red Mesa and on the east by Mesa Cuchilla.

Mesa Cuchilla (Knife Mesa) is not really a mesa at all, but rather a sharp ridge topping a cliff that rises a thousand feet from the valley floor. Gazing east from here I can see all the way to the snow-covered curve of Sandia Crest on the horizon.

Cabezon Peak from Red Mesa

    Looking west from the edge of Red Mesa, across a vast, arid landscape of mesas and canyons, I can see the squat, black lava plug known as Cabezon (Big Head) Peak on the horizon. The sandstone formations across which I walk were laid down when an inland sea covered this part of New Mexico. Over great spans of time, volcanic eruptions pushed up through the seabed in the form of basalt columns. As more eons passed, the sandstone eroded, exposing the harder volcanic rock as black monoliths like Cabezon Peak. My own life and concerns take on a quite different perspective when I witness evidence of the unimaginable span of time over which the earth developed.

    The two mesas, east and west of the syncline, rise to about 6700' and the lowest point in the trough is about 5700'. The whole formation is only about four miles wide, east to west, and perhaps eight miles north-south, from highway 550 to Jackrabbit Flats. Numerous small canyons cut through the trough and the sandstone is carved by wind and water into domes, towers, and odd knobs and fingers of rock known locally as "hoodoos."

The whole system is tilted to the South, which means it is wonderfully warmed by the winter sun. I have set out on hikes with the temperature at sunrise in the single digits and had lunch against a sun-warmed boulder in shirtsleeves.

While there are no official trails to guide me through this landscape, walking off trail is not difficult. Vegetation is sparse and the sandstone bedrock provides excellent footing. Pinon pines, junipers, stunted ponderosa pines, and a variety of desert shrubs anchor themselves in the thin soil and rock fissures, maintaining their hold through the fierce storms of winter and the drenching thunderstorms of late summer. Once, in a sheltered cove, where just a bit more water and soil had collected, I came upon a thriving cottonwood tree in a tiny, grassy meadow. Ponderosa pines generally grow at higher altitudes, with more moisture, and cottonwoods are common along rivers and streams, but slight variations of terrain and exposure in this desert land give higher elevation and streamside trees opportunities to move in and take hold.

It doesn't rain often here, and what precipitation falls drains away quickly, leaving channels and basins cut into the sandstone. Hiking one day after a night of rain, I found raincut channels flowing in shimmering rivulets and pools.

Water-carved sandstone

Some of these waterpockets can be quite deep and water preserved as ice by cold winter nights melts into mirror like reflecting pools during the day.

Reflections

There is a mysterious quality to this landscape, and on every hike there are surprises. Once while descending from Red Mesa through a steep canyon, my companions and I discovered that the floor of the canyon was made of blue limestone, full of tiny marine fossils, reminding us that this area was once covered by a shallow inland sea. Red sand drifted across the blue limestone bedrock creating intricate patterns in loops and swirls.

On another hike we came upon circular structures, two to four feet in diameter, made of large stones. The rocks are positioned to create a bowl in the center and are located on top of prominent boulders. There was no sign of fire within the bowls, so the structures could not have been fire rings. We puzzled over their origin and decided, since much of this hike is on Jemez Pueblo land, that they are most likely some sort of shrine created by the Pueblo People.

At the base of Red Mesa several mineral springs bubble up through the sandstone. Over centuries the springs have generated round mineral domes six to ten feet high. Animals large and small come here to drink, and it is clear from their droppings that the domes are strong enough to support the weight of a person. Mineral rich water still flows from round openings in some, while the springs of other domes have receded. From the tops of those structures where the water level has dropped I can look down to the corpses of small mammals and birds, trapped in the diminished waters when they entered the opening in search of precious moisture.

    The variety and complexity of this world astonishes me. Following a path I tend to pass through the world as an observer, going off the path I bring the mystery that is myself to the mystery that is the world. Dogen Zenji speaks of "fully engaging body and mind." I am much more likely to approach the world in this spirit when I leave the trail and in this intimate engagement boundaries dissolve and the world and myself arise together.

Never Alone
(Grand Canyon in Winter)

Keep walking,
though there's no place to get to.
Don't try to see through the distances.
That's not for human beings.
Move within,
but don't move
the way fear makes you move.

—Rumi

For many years I have wanted to walk to the bottom of the Grand Canyon from the South Rim. Summer is too hot for such a hike, so now, in February, I am about to descend the South Kaibab trail. I will stay overnight at Phantom Ranch, and the next day climb back out on the Bright Angel trail.

Friday

I seem suspended in timelessness as I wander along the South Rim, entranced by the sunrise this morning. The Canyon has been written about and photographed innumerable times, yet none of these images and descriptions prepared me for the awe and gratitude I feel as I stand on the rim, gazing into this immensity. The golden light of the rising sun creeps slowly down the formations below, further intensifying the colors of the rock and illuminating the few clouds above in the same warm glow.

Grand Canyon sunrise

Descending the South Kaibab Trail

I start down the South Kaibab trail about nine am, descending into this earth womb through the monumental rock formations. The only trees are wind twisted junipers tenaciously rooted in the red soil. The weather was clear at first, now clouds roll in and the wind picks up as the day progresses.

Two ravens

Stopping for lunch, two large ravens, perhaps a bonded pair, soon join me. Some birds, geese among them, form lifelong pair bonds. But ravens? It seems out of character to me, yet these intelligent birds are full of surprises. I like to think that they stay with me as I eat because they enjoy my companionship, but more likely they stay for the occasional tidbit I toss them.

I'm bunking with seven other men in a cabin at Phantom Ranch. Four of the men in these cramped but cheerful lodgings are brothers who made this trip in 1974 with their father. Their father is deceased, and the men, now middle aged, arranged this reunion, one of them bringing his young son.

We gather with the other guests, most of them down here for the first time, for a dinner of beef stew. The majority of the visitors are Brits and Europeans. One of my dorm mates is a Bulgarian, who is here with his wife and two young daughters. Some of these travelers are experienced hikers and backpackers, others are not used to strenuous hiking and are, as one of the brothers put it, "stove in." An urgent topic of conversation is the winter storm predicted for tomorrow afternoon and on into Sunday. Should we head out tomorrow morning, to get ahead of the bad weather, or stay an extra day and wait out the storm at the bottom?

Saturday

Several of us start out before dawn, lighting the trail with our headlamps. It is warm and pleasant here at the bottom, the few clouds above turning pink as we walk the River Trail and dawn gathers over the Colorado River. Heavier clouds begin to form and the sky darkens as we climb the Bright Angel Trail and we can see the storm approaching from the East.

The group I started with soon breaks up and I continue on alone. The weather remains warm and pleasant until about three miles from the top, when heavy snow begins falling. The visibility on the trail diminishes to 20 or 30 yards and the dramatic formations of the canyon become ghostly shapes looming in the storm.

Snowstorm

Under the heavy, windless snowfall a profound, enveloping silence descends over the canyon, broken occasionally by the calls of ravens. These shrewd birds have a remarkable repertoire of vocalizations, and as their varied voices echo through the canyon I imagine them reporting to each other on the progress of the storm and the location of tasty carcasses. Or perhaps it is the pair who joined me for lunch, reminding me that I am never really alone on my solitary hikes. The Bright Angel Trail is over nine miles from canyon floor to the South Rim. I reach the top after seven and a half hours of breaking trail through the fresh snow, tired, sore, and profoundly happy.

This trip epitomizes all I love about strenuous hiking in wild places. The sensory input is so marvelous and the physical engagement so demanding that there is very little of my mind left for pondering my life, questioning my relationships, or planning anything at all. I am in place in a way that is more complete than during any other activity. I do not strategize, except to plan the best way to get from where I am to the next waypoint. I do not calculate, except to recognize danger and to assess my limits. I am here and the place fills me. I give myself without constraint and without asking any more in return than just to be here.

The lights of Bright Angel Lodge, situated just a few feet from the rim, are a welcome sight as I reach the top. Fortunately the Lodge has a room available, and not wanting to drive home in the storm I will spend the night here.

Sunday

I awaken to wind blown snow, so no driving home this morning. I'll sit zazen before breakfast.

In zazen my conscious mind spontaneously arranges sensory impressions and thoughts into stories, just as it does in my active life. If I slip into sleep, my unconscious mind does the same, although these stories seem bizarre and incomprehensible to my conscious mind. Surrendering all stories to breathing, I cannot say who or what I am, only that, " I am." Here there are no categories, no descriptions, no stories. Here is where the "I" of my daily life takes refuge.

In Case 55 of *The Blue Cliff Record*, Zengen, a Zen monk, and Dogo, his teacher, visit a home to pay a condolence call on the family of a recently deceased man. While they are there, Zengen hits the coffin and says, "Alive or dead?"

Dogo: " Alive I won't say; dead, I won't say either.
Zengen: "Why won't you say?"
Dogo: "I won't say. I won't say."

The master won't say because any answer he might give would limit the moment and betray the intimacy. He won't say in order to push the questioning monk to an experience of "I am." To put the matter in temporal terms, when one moment dies another is born. We cling to some manifestations of birth/death and try to avoid or get rid of others. To fully accept the birth/death of each moment is liberation.

After breakfast I learn that stretches of I-40 are closed, due to blowing snow. I'll stay here another day—sit, read, maybe go for a walk along the rim if the storm lifts.

Entering a wild place, I invariably receive an unexpected gift. This trip has opened me to the beauty, transience, and poignancy of the world and my life. Standing on the rim of the Canyon, talking to Kathleen on my cell phone, I could not speak or hold back tears. Everywhere I see beauty. Everyone I encounter seems vulnerable, wanting to reach out for some kind of reassuring contact.

Sunlight and shadow on the canyon

Monday

The storm has lifted. In the intermittent sun and a light breeze, I walk west along the Rim Trail for a couple of miles. The sun piercing the clouds creates an ever changing pattern of light and shadow on the formations of the Canyon. A few hundred yards from the lodge and I am alone, breaking trail through the snow. I imagine that solitude on this trail is a rare occurrence, even in winter.

This has been an unusual day for me—I had no plans. I sat zazen at dawn, before lunch, before dinner, and before bed. I read and wandered along the rim trail through the fresh snow, taking photos of the play of sunlight and cloud shadow on the formations of the Canyon. I seem stripped of some protective carapace. I feel great affection and tenderness for everyone I encounter and everyone else seems dazed, happy, and tender as well.

Tuesday

Back in Santa Fe, I saw psychotherapy clients during the day, held dokusan (private interviews) with Zen students this evening, and caught up on world news. Back in my life, I am again faced with the anguish of sentient beings. After going to bed I awaken around two am with this anguish on my mind. The hour of the wolf. The distress of one particular woman, representing, I suppose, all the distress I encountered during the day, will not let me sleep. I do what I always do when I cannot sleep—I get up and sit zazen. I am never more grateful for my practice and for zazen than at these times.

I lead a life of engagement, which means a life in touch with suffering. The openness that I felt coming out of the canyon allows me to relate directly to this suffering. The refuge of zazen allows me to experience my True Nature, where there is neither suffering nor beings that suffer. There is just this, which needs nothing from what I imagine to be me.

> *No suffering, no cause or end to suffering;*
> *No path, no wisdom and no gain.*
> *No gain—thus Bodhisattvas live this Prajna Paramita*
> *With no hindrance of mind, no hindrance therefore no fear.*
> *Far beyond all such delusion, Nirvana is already here.*
> *—Prajna Paramita Heart Sutra*

Epilogue

> *The moon and sun are eternal travelers. Even the years wander on. Every day is a journey and the journey itself is home. From the earliest times there have always been some who perished along the road. Still, I have always been drawn by wind blown clouds into dreams of a lifetime of wandering.*
> —Basho

For many years before I began Zen practice in 1970, I found adventure, serenity, and joy backpacking in wilderness. As my Zen practice evolved I discovered there a similar release from the anxieties and complications of life. Now I regard these two practices as complementary paths toward liberation.

I hope through these photos and commentary I have succeeded in sharing with you a little of the joy and wholeness that I experience in my rambles through the wildlands, the deserts and mountains, of the Southwestern United States.

Happy Trails,
Musai Roshi